LAUGHING MATTERS

SCHOOL JOKES

Compiled by Pam Rosenberg
Illustrated by Patrick Girouard

Special thanks to Katie Cottrell for her assistance in compiling source materials.

Published in the United States of America by The Child's World®
PO Box 326, Chanhassen, MN 55317-0326
800-599-READ
www.childsworld.com

Acknowledgments
The Child's World®: Mary Berendes, Publishing Director

Editorial Directions, Inc.: E. Russell Primm, Editorial Director and Line Editor; Katie Marsico, Assistant Editor; Matthew Messbarger, Editorial Assistant; Susan Ashley, Proofreader

The Design Lab: Kathleen Petelinsek, Designer; Kari Thornborough, Page Production

Library of Congress Cataloging-in-Publication Data
Rosenberg, Pam.
   School jokes / compiled by Pam Rosenberg ; illustrated by Patrick Girouard.
      p. cm. — (Laughing matters)
   ISBN 1-59296-282-3 (library bound : alk. paper) 1. Schools—Juvenile humor. 2. Education—Juvenile humor. 3. Riddles, Juvenile. I. Girouard, Patrick. II. Title. III. Series.
   PN6231.S3R64 2005
   818'.602—dc22   2004016865

CAFETERIA JOKES

Where do young cows eat at school?
In the calf-eteria.

What happened to the vegetables that were misbehaving in the school cafeteria?
They found themselves in hot water.

Why did the cafeteria worker wear Rollerblades?
So she could serve fast food.

Why did the computer go to the school cafeteria?
It wanted a few bytes.

3

LANGUAGE ARTS JOKES

What happened when the English teacher's dictionary was stolen?
    She was at a loss for words.

What do you get when you cross the English department with the school cafeteria?
    Alphabet soup.

What happened to the student who swallowed the dictionary?
    The school nurse couldn't get a word out of him.

What do you get if you cross the alphabet with a spinning top?
    Dizzy spells.

What do elves learn in school?
    The elf-abet.

Why did the mailman take the alphabet?
    So he could deliver the letters.

Mom: My child is a genius. She has the most original ideas, hasn't she?
Teacher: Yes, especially when it comes to spelling.

COMPUTER JOKES

Why did the cat take a computer class?
It wanted to get hold of a mouse.

What did the pig put in the school computer?
Sloppy disks.

AT THE LIBRARY

Why did the caterpillar go to the library?
It wanted to become a bookworm.

Who guards the school library?
The bookkeeper.

MISCELLANEOUS JOKES

Why did the kids get wet going to school?
They were in a car pool.

Did you hear about the cross-eyed teacher?
She couldn't control her pupils.

What would you get if you crossed a vampire and a teacher?
Lots of blood tests.

What do you get when you cross a goat with a kangaroo?
A kid with a built-in schoolbag.

Why did the third grader bring a lightbulb to school?
She had a bright idea.

Why did the guitar leave music class?
Everyone kept picking on it.

8

Why did members of the drama club get sent to detention?
They kept acting up.

What's yellow, has wheels, and lies on its back?
A dead school bus.

Why did the student bring a ladder to school?
She was interested in higher education.

Is your teacher strict?
I don't know. I'm too scared to ask.

Knock Knock.
Who's there?
Don Juan.
Don Juan who?
Don Juan to go to school today.

9

Teacher: Does anyone know which month has 28 days in it?

Russell: All of them.

Teacher: Why are you writing on a piece of sandpaper?

Sarah: You told us to write a rough draft.

Pupil (on phone): My son has a bad cold and won't be able to come to school today.

School Secretary: Who is this?

Pupil: This is my father speaking.

Teacher: You missed school yesterday, didn't you?

Pupil: Not very much!

Sally: My teacher doesn't even know what a horse looks like.

Mom: That's impossible.

Sally: Well, I drew a picture of a horse and she asked me what it was.

HOMEWORK, TEST, AND REPORT CARD JOKES

Is it better to do your homework on a full stomach or an empty stomach?
It's better to do it on paper.

What grades did the pirate get in school?
High seas.

Why did the student glue himself to his report?
He was trying to stick to the subject.

What happened when the sailor saw his report card?
He got C sick.

Teacher, I don't think I deserve a zero on this test.
Neither do I, but it's the lowest mark I can think of.

11

Teacher: Where is your homework?
Jake: I lost it fighting this kid who said you weren't the best teacher in school!

What can you never make with poor penmanship? Straight As.

Mom: Sit down and show me your report card.
Son: I can't sit down. I just showed it to Dad.

Why was the little bird punished? It was caught peeping during a test.

Teacher: I take real pleasure in giving you a 90 on this test.
Matt: Then why don't you give me a 100 and really enjoy yourself?

Girl Monster: Mommy, the teacher said I was neat, pretty, and well behaved.
Mommy Monster: Don't worry, dear. You'll do better next time.

What kind of tests do witches take at school? Hex-aminations.

Why did the D student take his report card to the beach? He wanted to get it above C level.

Teacher: You copied from Katie's exam paper, didn't you?
Matt: How did you know?
Teacher: Katie's paper says, "I don't know," and your paper says, "Me neither!"

Teacher: This test is multiple choice.
Joseph: Then I choose not to take it!

13

THE PRINCIPAL'S OFFICE

Principal: This is the fifth time this week that you've been in my office. What do you have to say for yourself?
Nicholas: I'm glad it's Friday!

Teacher: I'm having trouble with one of my students.
Principal: What's the problem?
Teacher: Not only is he the worst-behaved child in class, he has a perfect attendance record.

Why was the voice teacher so good at baseball?
She had perfect pitch.

Why couldn't the elephant join the swim team?
He forgot his trunks.

Why did the basketball player start a fire?
The coach told him to warm the bench.

Why did the locomotive go to the gym?
It wanted to join the track team.

What would you get if you crossed an English teacher with the track team?
A run-on sentence.

Why did the doughnut join the basketball team?
To practice dunking.

Student: The doctor says I can't play football.
Coach: I could have told you that.

16

Why did the tiny ghost join the football team? He heard they could use a little school spirit.

TRADE SCHOOL

Is a hammer a useful tool in math?

No, but multi-pliers are.

What did the builder do his homework on?

Construction paper.

Why did the electrician go to school?

To study current events.

MATH JOKES

What do math teachers wear to ballet class?
    Two-twos.

How do you recognize math plants?
    They have square roots.

If you cut 2 apples and 3 pears into 10 pieces each, what would you have?
    Fruit salad.

What would you have if you had five apples in one hand and three in the other?
    Huge hands.

Why is 3 + 3 = 7 like your left foot?
    Because it's not right.

If you had 200 pennies, 100 nickels, and 75 quarters in your pockets, what would you have?
    Droopy pants.

Teacher: Now class, whatever I ask, I want you to all answer at once. How much is five plus four?
Class: At once!

Math Teacher: What is a polygon?
Student: A dead parrot.

What kind of food do math teachers like? Square meals.

Patrick: Mom, can you help me find the lowest common denominator in this problem?
Mom: Don't tell me they haven't found it yet. They were looking for it when I was in school!

SOCIAL STUDIES JOKES

Why did the history book go out so much? It had a lot of dates.

Teacher: Why does the Statue of Liberty stand in New York Harbor?
Judi: Because it can't sit down.

What are the small rivers that run into the Nile?
The juve-niles.

What do you call the first page of a geography book?
The table of continents.

Dad: Why aren't you doing well in history?
Daniel: Because the teacher keeps asking about things that happened before I was born!

Teacher: What's the difference between an American student and an English student?
Student: About 3,000 miles.

21

Geography Teacher: What's the most slippery country in the world?
Student: Greece.

History Teacher: When was the Great Depression?
Student: The last time I got my report card.

Geography Teacher: What has two humps and is found at the North Pole?
Student: A lost camel.

NORTH POLE

Why did the science teacher and her husband get divorced?
    They didn't have the right chemistry.

Science Teacher: Why do birds fly south in the winter?
Student: Because it's too far to walk.

Why did the baby go to chemistry class?
    To learn formulas.

What would you get if you crossed the geology department with the school band?
    Rock music.

About Patrick Girouard:

Patrick Girouard has been illustrating books for almost 15 years but still looks remarkably lifelike. He loves reading, movies, coffee, robots, a beautiful red-haired lady named Rita, and especially his sons, Marc and Max. Here's an interesting fact: A dog named Sam lives under his drawing board. You can visit him (Patrick, not Sam) at www.pgirouard.com.

About Pam Rosenberg:

Pam Rosenberg is a former junior high school teacher and corporate trainer. She currently works as an author, editor, and the mother of Sarah and Jake. She took on this project as a service to all her fellow parents of young children. At least now their kids will have lots of jokes to choose from when looking for the one they will tell their parents over and over and over again!

24